PICTURING SCOTLAND

FIFE, KINROSS
& CLACKMANNAN

NESS PUBLISHING

2 The south-east portion of Fife is known as the East Neuk and is famed for its picturesque harbours and golden sands that line the Firth of Forth. Elie, seen here, boasts perhaps the finest beach.

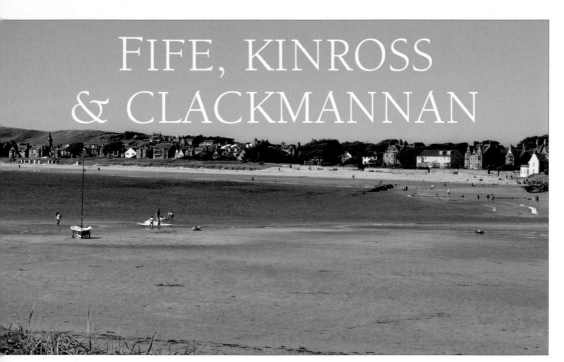

FIFE, KINROSS & CLACKMANNAN

See also pages 36-37.

Welcome to Fife, Kinross & Clackmannan!

That's quite a mouthful for a relatively small part of Scotland, but a look at a map of the country will bear out that these three regions sit well together. Although Kinross is, administratively, joined to Perthshire, geographically it sits between Fife to its east and Clackmannanshire to its west, while the Ochil Hills to the north separate it from Perthshire. Artefacts from Scotland's deep past and vestiges of its early history abound all the way from Clackmannan to St Andrews.

St Andrews is a story in itself: home of Scotland's oldest university, founded in 1413, it also gathers within its compact policies the remains of the largest cathedral in the land, a substantial and well-preserved castle, a delightful town centre of medieval origins, a world-famous golf course and magnificent beaches. The aerial picture opposite gives a sense of how some of these elements blend together around the focal point of the cathedral and the even earlier St Rule's Church. The earliest reference to the settlement which became St Andrews goes back to 747 when Irish annals record the death of the abbot Túathalán. That this event became a matter of record so far away is an indicator of the importance it must already have acquired. In the early medieval period it was known as Kilrymont, meaning 'church on the head of the king's mount (hill)', indicating there were royal associations as well as the ecclesiastical establishment. Legend has it that the relics of St Andrew were brought to the town from Greece in the 4th

An aerial view of the east end of St Andrews. Above the harbour are the cathedral precincts in which   5
the square form of St Rule's Tower is prominent.

century by St Rule. In due course the town's name changed to reflect its importance as a place of pilgrimage for those seeking St Andrew's blessing.

Over the course of time the Diocese of St Andrews became the home of Scotland's most important bishop. A suitably magnificent cathedral church was deemed necessary to complement this high status. Construction began in 1163 but due to a string of setbacks it was not consecrated until 1318. It housed the shrine of St Andrew, one of the most important pilgrimage places in western Christendom. Two-and-a-half centuries later, with the winds of reform blowing through the church, and following an inflammatory sermon by John Knox in 1559 at Holy Trinity Church, St Andrews, ruination of the cathedral (opposite) began.

A journey around these compact parts of Scotland takes longer than the mere mileage would suggest due to the almost continuous stream of points and places of interest. The East Neuk fishing ports compete with each other to present seaside vistas of

6 The surviving west tower of St Andrews Cathedral seen through an arch of the south transept.

matchless charm. In villages such as Falkland and Culross time seems to have stopped at a moment several centuries ago. The volume and variety of castles and palaces leaves the onlooker spoiled for choice and, in between the abundance of built landscape, the pastoral one stretches luxuriantly across the gently rolling landforms. Some major towns add their urban qualities to the roll call of points of call. Dunfermline is surprisingly historic and stands out in this category: King Malcolm III married Margaret there c.1070. Margaret then founded a priory that grew into the abbey which then became the burial place of many Scottish monarchs, including Robert the Bruce and Elizabeth, his Queen.

This book takes a roughly circular, clockwise tour that starts in St Andrews then follows Fife's southern coast where two of its most impressive structures await inspection – the mighty Forth Bridges; then to Clackmannanshire with its backdrop of the Ochil Hills and returning through Kinross to the central and northerly parts of Fife. It's quite a journey . . .

The tomb of King Robert the Bruce in Dunfermline Abbey. 7

8   The top of St Rule's Tower provides the best viewpoint in St Andrews. The two main thoroughfares of South Street (left of centre) and North Street (right of centre) converge on the cathedral grounds.

The castle can be seen on the right and the golf links are in the distance above various university buildings. St Salvator's Tower dominates North Street.

10 St Andrews' sunrise. The famous harbour wall, promenading place for generations of students, projects into the sea. On the right, fishing creels await their next use.

This is the reverse view, from the harbour wall, with St Rule's Tower and the remaining cathedral 11 towers on the skyline.

12 Now within the cathedral precincts: a small part of the nave of St Rule's Church remains attached to the tower. This building is hard to date, but is generally thought to be from around 1123.

St Andrews Castle. Although it dates back to the 12th century, most of what remains is more recent. **13**
The fore tower on the left is from around 1390 and much of the rest is 16th century.

14 Left: the 15th-century tower and chapel of St Salvator's College on North Street. Right: St Andrews motto and crest loosely means 'While there's life there's hope'.

Going through the door in St Salvator's tower (opposite) leads into the college quad where one is **15** met by a scene like this – depending on the season of course.

16 The commercial heart of St Andrews is located along Market Street, which runs between, and parallel to, North and South Streets. This view looks east towards the west tower of the cathedral.

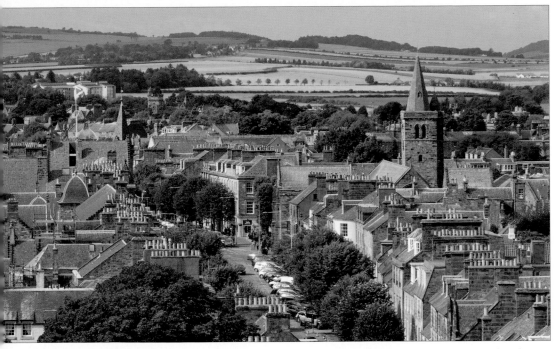

To locate the places on the following pages we look west along South Street. The spire of Holy **17** Trinity Church is on the right, opposite St Mary's College. West Port is at the far end.

18 From South Street, a glimpse into St Mary's College quad. Founded as the University's School of Divinity in 1539 by Archbishop David Beaton, it continues in this role today.

Left: the scant remains of Blackfriars Chapel, South Street, once part of a Dominican friary. **19**
Right: the entrance to Holy Trinity Church, the present structure of which dates from 1907-9.

20 Early on a summer Sunday morning, peace still reigns in Church Square, with the colourful gardens of Holy Trinity Church and a variety of architectural styles.

At the end of South Street, West Port incorporates a wealth of carved features. Built in 1587, it was **21** renovated in 1843 at which time the side arches were added.

22 The Royal and Ancient Golf Club of St Andrews goes back to 1754. The links extend out from the famous Club House. The bridge in the foreground is a favourite spot for wedding photographs.

St Andrews west beach goes all the way up the sandbar that forms the south side of the River Eden **23** estuary. Across the estuary lies the Tentsmuir Forest.

24 A complete change of scene now as we leave St Andrews and investigate the East Neuk with its famously pretty coastal panoramas. St Monans' harbour is backed by uniformly quaint cottages.

Like all such ports, fishing now plays less of a part in the local economy but continues on a modest scale, as can be seen by the creels stacked up on the pier.

26 Away from the coast there is plenty to see. Kellie Castle stands a couple of miles inland from St Monans. Built in the 14th century it is noted for its plaster ceilings and painted panelling.

Scotland's Secret Bunker near Crail is certainly a unique attraction, giving visitors the chance to visit **27** the underground command centre built in the 1950s due to the threat of nuclear war.

28 Crail is the most easterly of the East Neuk villages and is delightfully picturesque. Left: spring flowers in Marketgate, opposite The Old House, underline the point. Right: harbour cottages.

Crail is the oldest of the East Neuk burghs, growing up around the harbour and (long gone) castle. **29**
King James II reputedly described it as 'A fringe of gold on a beggar's mantle'.

30 West of Crail, Anstruther continues the theme, albeit on a larger scale, with a harbour that is now a marina as well as a working port. The Scottish Fisheries Museum is on the waterfront.

Away from the harbour it has one of those beaches that just begs to be explored. Judging from its **31** uniform appearance, the ancient sea-defence wall seems to have survived well.

32 Pittenweem comes next – the name means 'place of the cave', a reference to the cave in Cove Wynd (left) that St Fillan used as a church in the 8th century. Right: Pittenweem harbour wall.

Pittenweem is now the busiest of the East Neuk fishing ports. It still provides a base for larger **33** vessels, a goodly number of which can be seen in the inner harbour.

34 Now we return to St Monans, where the former boatyard slipway now finds alternative use displaying some creative floral arrangements – a good way to retire your leaky wellingtons!

It's not hard to work out how the village got its name. St Monan did not found this church but was **35** buried here (or part of him anyway!) and a shrine built to venerate his memory.

36 Elie's main claim to fame is its wonderful beach. In contrast to the panoramic view on pages 2-3, here is a different perspective on a resort that grew with the coming of the railway in 1863.

This aerial view adds another dimension. The earliest part of the village can be discerned in the rectangle of houses in the lower middle part of the picture next to the beach.

38 And now for something completely different! Moving inland to the new town of Glenrothes, a distinctive and diverse collection of public art cannot fail to grab the attention.

A huge variety of work from 1965 to the present is spread across the whole town. Facing page: **39**
'Giant Irises' rivals the height of the lamp posts. Above: 'Heritage' is framed by autumn colour.

40 Of course, being in Scotland, a castle is never far away and here, in the countryside east of Glenrothes, is Balgonie Castle. The tower, the oldest still standing intact in Fife, was built for

Sir Thomas Sibbald and is regarded as one of the finest 14th-century towers in Scotland.

42 Left: returning to the coast at Dysart near Kirkcaldy, the 13th-century St Serf's Tower stands behind houses on Pan Ha'. Right: in Kirkcaldy itself, architectural detail in Kirk Wynd.

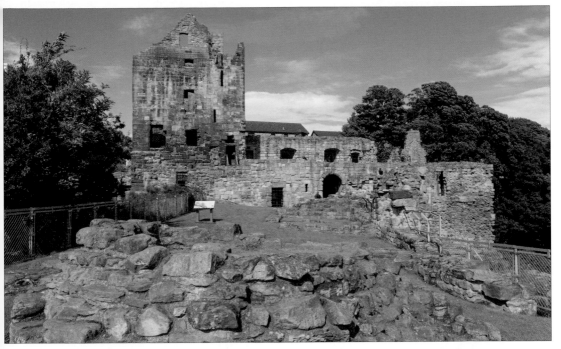

Kirkcaldy's Ravenscraig Castle is one of the earliest artillery forts in Scotland. The west tower **43** (on the left), was the residence of James II's widow, Queen Mary of Gueldres.

44 Adam Smith, economist, philosopher and author of *The Wealth of Nations*, was born in Kirkcaldy in 1723. This is the St Brycedale Campus of the college which is named after him.

Continuing southwards along the coast, Kinghorn bay provides a pleasing early-morning image. **45**
The harbour has seen more active times; ferries used to cross over to Edinburgh.

46 The resort of Burntisland is spread out around the headland that was the focus of the original settlement. The island of Inch Keith lies in the Firth of Forth, with the Lothians beyond.

Now viewed across the bay from Petty Cur, Burntisland's Rossend Castle peeps through the trees 47
while the town's buildings cluster around The Links, where the fair is in town.

48 A little further west is Aberdour. Here, St Fillans is one of those ancient churches which, despite much rebuilding and restoration through the years, still makes the visitor feel they are connecting

with the eternal. The welcoming porch (opposite) leads to an especially atmospheric interior in which the relative darkness of the nave contrasts with the lit chancel, above.

50 Standing next to St Fillans Church, 12th-C. Aberdour Castle is arguably the oldest standing stone castle in Scotland. The terraced garden dates to the 16/17th centuries. Inset: the castle sundial.

Inchcolm lies in the Firth of Forth off Aberdour. Its abbey comprises the best-preserved group of **51** monastic buildings in Scotland. The island can be reached by boat from South Queensferry.

52 The two most iconic structures of modern times in Fife are the Forth Bridges. The 1.5 mile/2.5 km road bridge shows off its graceful curves to good effect in this evening view.

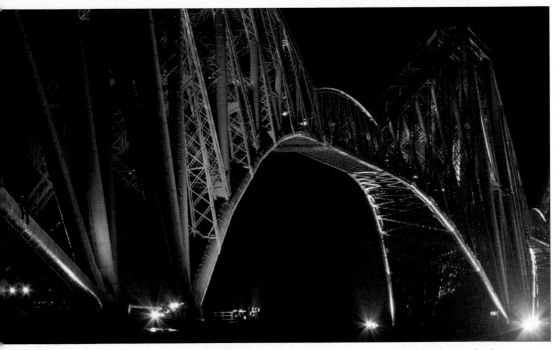

However, it is the form, complexity and massive proportions of the rail bridge that draws the longest 53
stares and deeper admiration. By night, the lighting makes it even more impressive.

54 And so to Dunfermline. The priory founded by Queen Margaret later became an Abbey and James VI added a palace, some remains of which are in the foreground, with the gatehouse above.

The abbey church contains both 12th- and 19th-century parts. Seen from Lady Halkett's Garden at **55** Abbot House (see pages 60-61), the nearer, towered end is the 19th-century building.

56 The Forth Rail Bridge does rather demand the panoramic treatment, especially when backlit by the dawn. Begun in 1883 and opened in 1890, it was the world's first major steel bridge. It consumed

54,000 tons of steel and a staggering 6.5 million rivets. Up to 4,000 men were employed on its construction. It carries 180-200 trains a day.

58 Dedicated in 1821, the 'new' Dunfermline Abbey was, in effect, a rebuild of the original structure. Visually, the focal point of the light and airy interior is the Great East Window, seen in this view.

O the GLORY of GOD and in memory of Mr and Mrs Jone Father Hemlands Dunterline

Another magnificent stained-glass work is the Malcolm and Margaret Memorial Window which **59** depicts their marriage (see introduction). It was installed and dedicated in 1933.

60 The wonderful Abbot House has its origins in the 15th century. Much added to through the years and recently restored, today it houses a first-rate heritage centre. Tours of the house explain

Dunfermline's history with the help of room settings like this one. One of its former residents was herbalist Lady Anne Halkett, to whom the garden seen on p.55 is dedicated.

62 Left: amongst much interesting architecture in Dunfermline is the finely detailed Mercat Cross.
Right: the City Chambers' tower blends Gothic, French and Scots Baronial architectural styles.

Pittencrieff Park, or 'The Glen' as it is more commonly known by locals, was bought in 1902 by **63**
Dunfermline's most famous son Andrew Carnegie, who then gifted it to the town and its people.

64 On the coast west of Dunfermline is Culross, one of the most remarkable villages in Scotland. The buildings seen here give us a clue as to why. Centre stage is the Town House of 1626.

Perhaps even more stunning is Culross Palace, not a royal one but the home of local mining **65** magnate Sir George Bruce. The 16th/17th-century time capsule that is Culross owes much to him.

66 When its prosperity declined, the village and its people had no resources to update or modernise. So Culross remains in that moment. Ironically, its troubles then are the key to its revival now.

Climbing the wynd (lane) opposite is the way to Culross Abbey. Above is the interior of the Abbey Church (now the Parish Church), looking from the north transept into the chancel.

68 Clackmannanshire is at the western extremity of this tour. The former county town of Clackmannan is a pleasant backwater that boasts much of interest including the Tolbooth tower seen here.

Left: Clackmannan's name comes from the ancient boulder on top of this stone pillar: the 'clack' or **69** stone of Manau, a Celtic sea-god. Right: Clackmannan Tower stands in fields outside the town.

70 Alloa is now the principal town of Clackmannanshire. Left: one of the town's 'Sentinels', arms raised in welcome? Right: interesting architectural fusion at the redeveloped Kilncraigs Mill.

And of course, there is a castle! Alloa Tower used to be the focal point of a much larger complex, at its zenith one of the most impressive palaces in Scotland. Open to the public in summer.

72 The traditional county of Clackmannanshire was Scotland's smallest and, in these days of Unitary
Authorities, is the second smallest of those. Its rural side is captured here looking west, with

Clackmannan astride its low hill on the left. Clackmannan Tower can just be made out. Towards the right, Dumyat is the hill at the western end of the Ochils.

74 Left: Menstrie is one of the villages at the foot of the Ochil Hills, where Andy Scott's sculpture of a rather curious creature adds interest. Right: the Murray Clock in Tillicoultry.

The Ochil Hills form an imposing backdrop to Clackmannanshire, running west to east the length 75
of the county. The highest point is Ben Cleuch, 721m/2365ft, seen here towering above Tillicoultry.

76 Continuing east we reach Dollar where Castle Campbell is dramatically situated above Dollar Glen. This 15th-century fortress was the lowland stronghold of the powerful Campbell earls of Argyll.

Left: eastwards into Kinross, drama of the natural kind is encountered at Rumbling Bridge, where 77 the River Devon has carved a deep gorge. Right: The Devil's Mill waterfall, further upstream.

78 Loch Leven occupies a substantial amount of Kinross-shire. Mary, Queen of Scots, was imprisoned in the castle on the island in the foreground. Beyond are the snow-clad Lomond Hills.

Loch Leven is rich in wildlife and the RSPB's Vane Farm Reserve is situated on the southern shore. **79**
In autumn, flocks of Pink-footed geese gather here after their migration from Iceland.

80 While the Lomond Hills are mostly composed of sandstone and limestone, the two summits of East and West Lomond are volcanic in origin. West Lomond is seen here from East Lomond.

In contrast, the view to the north and east takes in the plains of northern Fife. At bottom right is the **81** historic village of Falkland, which rivals Culross in the time capsule stakes.

82 Now we zoom in on Falkland to pick out the jewel in its crown, Falkland Palace. Looking down from above gives a good idea of the extent of the palace – a favourite haunt of Stuart monarchs.

The 'classic' view of the palace as seen from within the village: James IV and James V transformed the original castle on this site into the Renaissance palace we see today.

84 Naturally, the gardens are spectacular too, with herbaceous borders, Jacobean herb garden and ancient orchard. The oldest Real (or Royal) Tennis court in Britain can be found here too.

The centre of Falkland. The quality and volume of its historic buildings is such that in 1970 the **85** village became Scotland's first conservation area. It has 28 listed buildings.

86 Falkland has that blend of uniformity-with-difference that conspires to produce such pleasing scenes. Here, at the west end of High Street, different colour schemes blend beautifully.

A few miles east of Falkland, the countryside around the village of Ceres typifies rural Fife. **87**
The village probably gets its name from an early Christian martyr by the name of St Cyr.

88 A brief bit of backtracking now to take a last look at a beautiful view. From Vane Hill viewpoint on the RSPB Reserve, here is an evening panorama of Loch Leven and the Lomond Hills. These hills

form an island of upland at the western end of Fife where it meets Kinross.

90 Situated close to Ceres, Hill of Tarvit is one of Scotland's finest Edwardian mansion houses, replete with a splendid collection of antiques, furniture, Chinese porcelain and superb paintings.

The old market town of Cupar lies in the heart of the Howe of Fife. It has a full complement of **91** grandiose buildings, as seen here in Cross Gate, but then it was Fife's county town for centuries.

92 Left: Cupar's Burgh Chambers, built 1815-17, stands at the corner of Cross Gate and St Catherine Street. Right: Cupar's War Memorial is a particularly striking example with its huge angel.

The War Memorial is at one of the entrances to Cupar's Haugh Park, where a programme of concerts 93 is held at the bandstand at certain times of year.

94 With our journey almost complete, here is Newport-on-Tay on the north Fife coast, viewed from Dundee. Beyond is Tentsmuir Forest and Eden Mouth, first seen from St Andrews back on p.23.

And finally, in Leuchars, is St Athernase Church, built c.1183-87. The Romanesque chancel and **95** apse (the right-hand end) are amongst the best Norman work in Britain.

Published 2013 by Ness Publishing, 47 Academy Street, Elgin, Moray, IV30 1LR.
Phone 01343 549663   www.nesspublishing.co.uk

All photographs © Colin Nutt except pp.5, 37 & 78 © Guthrie Aerial Photography; p.51 © Bob Marshall;
p.79 © Laurie Campbell

Text © Colin Nutt
ISBN 978-1-906549-24-4

Front cover: St Andrews; p.1: Pends Gate, St Andrews; p.4: statue of Jimmy Shand in Auchtermuchty; this page: Eider Duck at Petty Cur; back cover: Lindores Loch

For a list of websites and phone numbers please turn over > > > >

Websites and phone numbers (where available) for principal places featured in this book in alphabetical order:

Abbot House Heritage Centre: www.abbothouse.co.uk (T) 01383 733266
Aberdour Castle: www.historic-scotland.gov.uk (T) 01383 860519
Adam Smith College: www.adamsmith.ac.uk (T) 01592 223535
Alloa Tower: www.nts.org.uk (T) 0844 493 2129
Balgonie Castle: www.balgoniecastle.co.uk (T) 01592 753103
Castle Campbell: www.historic-scotland.gov.uk (T) 01259 742408
Clackmannan: www.clacksweb.org.uk
Culross: www.nts.org.uk (T) 0844 493 2189
Cupar: www.cupartown.co.uk
Dunfermline: www.visitdunfermline.com
Dunfermline Abbey: www.dunfermlineabbey.co.uk (T) 01383 724586
Dunfermline Palace and Abbey: www.historic-scotland.gov.uk (T) 01383 739026
East Neuk: www.eastneukwide.co.uk
Falkland Palace: www.nts.org.uk (T) 0844 493 2186
Fife: www.fifedirect.org.uk
Forth Bridges: www.forthbridges.org.uk
Glenrothes Town Art: www.historic-scotland.gov.uk
Hill of Tarvit Mansion House: www.nts.org.uk (T) 0844 493 2185
Inchcolm Abbey: www.historic-scotland.gov.uk (T) 01383 823332
Kellie Castle: www.nts.org.uk (T) 0844 493 2184